# My First
# Bible Stories

Illustrations by Leighton Noyes

## STAR FIRE BOOKS

Publisher and Creative Director: Nick Wells
Illustrations: Leighton Noyes
Text: Ann Pigeon
Editorial: Sara Robson
Art Director: Mike Spender
Layout Design: Jake
Digital Design and Production: Chris Herbert

ISBN 978 1 84451 709 1

10 9 8 7 6 5 4 3 2

12 11 10 09 08



First published in 2008 by
STAR FIRE BOOKS
Crabtree Hall, Crabtree Lane,
Fulham, London SW6 6TY, United Kingdom
www.star-fire.co.uk

Star Fire is part of the Foundry Creative Media Company Ltd.

© The Foundry 2008

Printed in Malaysia

A copy of the CIP data for this book is available from the British Library upon request.

**Publisher's Note**

There are many different versions of these Bible Stories, from many different sources. Different parts of the world, even different parts of the same country have traditions with very similar subjects, which were written down over many hundreds of years. The versions in this book represent a simplified view of these popular classic Bible Stories.

# Contents

# The Creation of Heaven and Earth

In the very beginning, when all was darkness, God created light, and made the day and the night. On the second day, he created the sky. On the third day, he created the earth, with all its bountiful plants, and vast seas. On the fourth day, he created the sun, the moon and the stars. On the fifth day, God made the creatures of the seas and skies.

On the sixth day, he made the living creatures of the land, and from the dust a man and a woman, whom he named Adam and Eve. On the seventh day, he had a rest.

# The Garden of Eden

God made a special garden for Adam and Eve, called Eden. In this garden were the lushest fruits and the most beautiful birds and creatures. Adam and Eve were very happy here. But there was one tree whose fruit God forbade them to eat. This was called the Tree of Knowledge. He warned them that if they ate from it, he would send them away from Eden. With so many other fruits in the garden, Adam and Eve never gave it a second thought.

# The Serpent

One day, when Eve was gathering berries, a snake slid over to her and started asking her about the Tree of Knowledge. Why didn't she and Adam eat the fruit? What harm could it do? What a silly rule God had made! It was probably the most delicious fruit in the garden! From that moment, Eve could not stop thinking about the Tree of Knowledge – until she picked a fruit and took it home to Adam.

They each had a bite and all at once felt unhappy. They couldn't hide from God, who had seen. Because they had broken their promise not to eat from the Tree of Knowledge, God cast them from the Garden of Eden.

# Noah's Ark

Noah was a man with a wife and three sons. He was kind and good and God loved him. God warned Noah that a flood would sweep the earth and that Noah should build an ark – an enormous boat. On this boat, Noah should bring all his family – his wife, his sons and their wives – and two of every animal of land, sea and sky. They would be safe on this boat until the floods had gone away.

11

# The Flood

It rained for forty days and forty nights. The whole earth was covered by water, even the highest mountain. The ark rose up with the waters, safe from the flood. When finally the water began to go down, Noah sent a dove from the boat, to see if dry ground was near. At first the bird returned with nothing, as it could not land anywhere. The next time the dove was sent, it returned with a leaf from an olive tree. This showed Noah that it was safe for the boat to land.

# Dry Land

All the creatures came down from the ark and found their place on land, and in sea and sky. Noah and his family farmed the earth and his sons and their wives had many children. God made a promise to Noah that He would never again bring such a flood to the earth. And to seal his promise, God created the rainbow.

# David and Goliath

There was once a boy named David, who lived in Israel. He was a shepherd, and spent his days looking after the sheep in the hills of this land. David was a brave and strong boy who loved to be outside. But one day David's life changed, when the people of his country began to fight a nation of people called the Philistines. David's big brothers went to fight in this war, but David remained behind to take care of the sheep.

# The Mighty Giant

One day, Jesse, David's father, asked him to take a bag of corn and ten loaves of bread to his brothers. When David arrived at the camp, high on a mountain, he found his brothers. On the other mountain across the valley, where the Philistines had their camp, stood a mighty giant, Goliath. He was covered in the strongest armour, from head to foot. Every day he would come to the edge of the mountain and shout across the valley at the soldiers of Israel: **'Send me a man so I may fight him!'** But the soldiers were too afraid.

# Victory

David, who was the youngest, and not even a soldier, said to all the men in the camp, 'Why do you not dare to fight the giant?'

'There is no one strong enough!' they all replied.

'I will fight this man,' said David, 'because God is on our side.'

David did not want to wear any armour, but instead went to a little stream, where he found five smooth stones. He found his sling and walked out to meet the giant. Goliath laughed at David, who was only a boy. But David swung the sling, and the stone went flying out and hit the giant on his head, the one place where his armour did not protect him. Goliath fell down, defeated, and brave David was rewarded by Saul, the King of Israel.

# The Birth of Jesus

A young woman named Mary, who lived in a place called Nazareth, was visited by the angel Gabriel. She was very afraid at this vision, but the angel told her that she had been blessed with a special task. Gabriel brought a message from God to say that Mary would bear a son and that she would name him Jesus. He would be the Son of God.

A carpenter named Joseph was soon to be Mary's husband, and he was sad that Mary's son would not be his own. But an angel came to Joseph too and told him that Jesus would grow into a very special man, and he had been sent to Mary and Joseph by God.

# To Bethlehem

Mary and Joseph had to travel from Nazareth to a place named Bethlehem. Mary was very close to having her baby. When they reached Bethlehem, they could not find anywhere to stay as all the inns were full. One innkeeper felt sorry for Mary and Joseph and let them spend the night in his stable, which was warm and clean. The child was born that night and they named him Jesus.

# Shepherds Watch Their Flocks

That same night an angel appeared to some shepherds watching their flocks on the hills outside Bethlehem. The angel told the shepherds that Christ had been born. And then a great host of angels appeared, who said: '**Glory to God in the highest, and on earth peace and good will toward men.**' The shepherds went down from the hills to visit the baby, whom they found in a manger. And from the east came three wise men bearing gifts. They had followed a star that guided them to where Jesus lay in his crib.

# The Good Samaritan

Once upon a time, there was a man who was walking along the
roadside from Jerusalem heading to Jericho, which was a full day or
two of walking. He was very poor and very weak. During his journey
he fell down by the roadside when he could not walk any further.
The first person who found this man was a priest, but he crossed
the road and would not help the man.

# A Second Chance

About an hour or so later, another man was walking down the road.
He slowed down and walked a little closer to the man, but then he
too kept walking without helping him. Even though the man needed
their help, neither of these men would stop to look after him.

# A Kind Deed

The third person to find the man went immediately to help him. He felt very sorry for this poor man. He lifted him up and put him on his donkey and took him to a place where he could be looked after. This man became known as the Good Samaritan, as he helped a stranger when all the other people would not help. He was very kind.